Dearly, Nearly, Insincerely

What Is an Adverb?

To Elio, Gina, and Vince who get
along swimmingly   —B.P.C.

For Sari   —B.G.

Adverb: A word
that describes
when, how, where,
how often, and
how much.

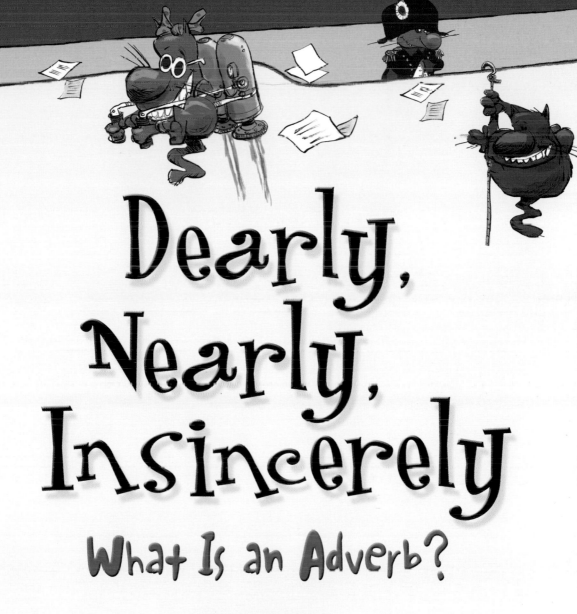

Dearly, Nearly, Insincerely

What Is an Adverb?

by Brian P. Cleary

illustrated by Brian Gable

M MILLBROOK PRESS / MINNEAPOLIS

They often help describe the verbs,

Like, *patiently* plant
peas and herbs.

PEAS

Adverbs will frequently end in "L-Y,"

As in viciously, ultra-suspiciously sly.

Adverbs add character, sizzle, and fizz

To your phrase or your sentence, whatever it is!

Frankly, this hot dog just couldn't be better.

Sheepishly, Fred found he'd ruined his sweater.

If they tell us **how**,
they're an
"adverb of manner,"

Like, **slowly** this summer,
my sister got tanner.

First, I was tired,

then, I was
woozy,

Next, I began
feeling sleepy
and snoozy.

They modify **adverbs**, like, she sang *quite* nicely.

Or he speaks so **swiftly** but **very** precisely.

Presently, pleasantly, properly praise.

Speedily, sometimes quite greedily, graze.

Adverbs, you'll find,
give the adjectives zip!

As in foolishly frisky

and
famously hip—

Bitterly angry, bitingly cold,

Brilliantly burgundy, shockingly old.

The adjective's "good,"
the **adverb** is "well."

So now that
you know that,
you're able to tell

That **well's** how you felt,
and good was your day.

Yes, **well** is a
very deep subject,
I'd say!

Dearly, nearly, insincerely,

Daily, weekly, monthly, yearly,

Truly, deeply, sadly, badly—

TRULY

DEEPLY

SADLY

BADLY

I tell you these are adVerbs, gladly.

And so are
sleekly and
uniquely,

Bravely,
boldly,

coldly, meekly.

So, what is an **adVerb?**

Do you know?

ABOUT THE AUTHOR & ILLUSTRATOR

BRIAN P. CLEARY is the author of several other picture books, including A Mink, a Fink, a Skating Rink: What Is a Noun?, To Root, to Toot, to Parachute: What Is a Verb?, Hairy, Scary, Ordinary: What Is an Adjective?, and Under, Over, By the Clover: What Is a Preposition?

BRIAN GABLE is the illustrator of Under, Over, By the Clover: What Is a Preposition? He lives in Toronto, Ontario, where he works as a political cartoonist.

Millbrook Press, a division of Lerner Publishing Group
241 First Avenue North, Minneapolis, MN 55401 U.S.A.

Website address: www.lernerbooks.com

Library of Congress Cataloging-in-Publication Data

Cleary, Brian P., 1959—
　　Dearly, nearly, insincerely : what is an adverb? / by Brian P. Cleary;
　　illustrated by Brian Gable.
　　　　p.　cm. — (Words are categorical)
　　Summary: Rhyming text and illustrations present numerous examples of
adverbs and their functions.
　　ISBN: 0—87614—924—7 (lib. bdg. : alk. paper)
　　1. English language—Adverb—Juvenile literature. [1. English language—
Adverb.] I. Gable, Brian, 1949—　II. Title.
PE1325 .C57　2003
428.2—dc21
2002003012

Printed in China
7　8　9　10　11　12　— LP — 10　09　08　07　06　05